Rookie
Read-About Science®

Energy from the Sun

By Allan Fowler

Consultants

Linda Cornwell, Learning Resource Consultant,
Indiana Department of Education

Fay Robinson, Child Development Specialist

◀P Children's Press®
A Division of Grolier Publishing
New York   London   Hong Kong   Sydney
Danbury, Connecticut

Project Editor: Downing Publishing Services
Designer: Herman Adler Design Group
Photo Researcher: Caroline Anderson

Library of Congress Cataloging-in-Publication Data

Fowler, Allan.
    Energy from the sun / by Allan Fowler.
      p. cm. – (Rookie read-about science)
    Includes index.
    Summary: Defines energy and examines how energy from the sun provides
us with heat, light, plants, food, and other things necessary for life on Earth.
    ISBN 0-516-20432-7 (lib. bdg.)   0-516-26255-6 (pbk.)
    1. Solar energy—Juvenile literature. [l. Solar energy.] I. Title. II. Series
TJ810.3.F69   1997   96-47000
333.792'3–dc21   CIP
                                     AC

   13 14 15 R 06 05

Has any grownup ever asked you, "Where do you get all that energy?"

Energy is what you need
a lot of to run around and
play and climb and jump
and shout.

Energy is what you run
out of when you get tired.

Energy is what makes
things move. It makes
machines do their work.
It gives us heat and light.

Toasters and TV sets and
computers run on a type
of energy called electricity.

Where do you get *your* energy?

You get it from the food
you eat. Much of what
you eat is plant life.

From plants we get
fruits . . . vegetables . . .

and the wheat, corn, or
other grains from which
bread and cereals are made.

Plants themselves need
food to live and grow.

From the simplest blade
of grass to the tallest
tree, each plant makes
its own food.

A plant makes its food
out of water and air. But
something else is needed
to turn water and air into
food for a plant.

What is needed is energy.

This energy comes from
the sun. It is in every
beam of sunlight that
shines down on Earth.

Without the sun's energy, plants could not grow— and you would have nothing to eat.

But what about meat, milk, eggs, and fish? Don't those come from animals?

Yes, they do. They come from animals that eat plant life. Think of cows grazing on grass.

The sun's energy works
inside a plant to make
food for the plant.

And as this happens, the plant releases a bit of a gas called oxygen into the air.

Most of the oxygen in the air around us comes from plants in this way.

If there were no oxygen in the air, we couldn't breathe.

So every breath of
air you take . . .

every bite of food
you eat . . .

depends on energy
from the sun.

You even use energy that came from the sun way back when dinosaurs roamed the Earth.

23

Great forests of plant life grew on this energy. Then, over a long, long time, the plants were buried —

and slowly changed
into coal or petroleum
or natural gas.

Cars, trucks, and buses run on the energy in gasoline, which comes from petroleum.

Houses and other buildings
may be heated by the energy
in coal or natural gas.

Whether you walked to school today . . . or rode in a car or bus . . . energy from the sun helped you get there.

"Where do you get all that energy?" From the sun! No wonder you have so much of it.

Words You Know

Energy

sunlight

jump

play

electricity

fruit

grain

cows

milk

plant life

coal

gasoline

Index

About the Author

Allan Fowler is a free-lance writer with a background in advertising.
Born in New York, he lives in Chicago now and enjoys traveling.

Photo Credits

Photographs ©: Photo Researchers: 25, 31 bottom left (Brian Brake), 10, 11, 30
bottom right, 31 top left (Mark C. Burnett), 23 (Chris Butler), 24 (Ted Clutter),
3, 30 top right (Tim Davis), 26, 31 bottom right (David R. Frazier), 7, 30
bottom left (Spencer Grant), 4, 30 middle left (Jeff Isaac Greenberg), 18 (John
Kaprielian), 15 (Brock May), 17, 31 top right (Garry D. McMichael), 20 (Jerry
Wachter); PhotoEdit: 29 (Myrleen Cate), 9, 16, 31 middle left (David Young-
Wolf); Photosynthesis/Ellen B. Senisi: 5, 6, 13, 24 inset, 31 middle right;
Superstock, Inc.: 8, 28; Tony Stone Images: cover (Paul Fletcher); Valan Photos:
27 (Michel Julien), 14 (Albert Kuhnigk), 30 top left (Albert Kuhnigk).